# MACHINES RULE!

# ON THE SEA

## Steve Parker

A+

**Smart Apple Media**

Smart Apple Media
P.O. Box 3263
Mankato, Minnesota 56002

Printed in the United States.

Published by arrangement with the Watts Publishing
Group Ltd, London.


Library of Congress Cataloging-in-Publication Data

Parker, Steve, 1976-
  On the sea / Steve Parker.
      p. cm.—(Machines rule!)
  Includes bibliographical references and index.
  Summary: "Covers a wide selection of machines used on the
sea, from submarines to sailboats, outlining how they work and
what they are used for"–Provided by publisher.
  ISBN 978-1-59920-286-0 (hardcover)
  1. Boats and boating—Juvenile literature. 2. Ships—Juvenile
literature. I. Title.
  VM150.P348 2010
  623.82–dc22
                                                      2008044507


Editor: Jeremy Smith
Editor-in-chief: John C. Miles
Design: Billin Design Solutions
Art director: Jonathan Hair
Picture credits: Aston Martin: 6, 10, 11r, 11br. Bugatti: OFC, 4-
5, 8-9. Corbis/Bruce Benedict/Transtock: 11b. Ducatti: 19c & b.
istockphoto: OFC bl & br, 7t, 7c, 7b, 12 all, 13t, 13b, 22 all,
23t, 23b, 24 all, 25c. www.JayOhrberg.com: 13c. Shutterstock:
11t, 14b, 14t, 15c, 15b, 16, 17 all, 19t, 20-21 all, 23tr, 25 all,
26-27 all, 28-29 all.

Words in **bold** or ***bold italics*** can be found in the glossary on
page 28.

9 8 7 6 5 4 3 2 1

# CONTENTS

# Powerboat Racing

It's rough, tough, fast, furious—and very wet! Huge waves batter the boat. Wind and water sting your face as opponents try to speed past. Powerboat racing gets boats up to speeds of 65 miles per hour (105 km/h) to 190 miles per hour (305 km/h) as they cruise through a racing circuit on the water.

Powerboats look like speedboats, but move much faster. The boat's **hull** has to be strong enough to stand up to powerful waves.

*strong hull*

# THAT'S INCREDIBLE

The world speed record on water was set in 1978 by Ken Warby in the *Spirit of Australia* speedboat, at 317 mph (511 km/h).

# Stats and Facts

**P1 Evolution Class Powerboat Racer**

**Makers: Various**

**Length: 36-102 ft (11-31 m)**

**Width: 8-11.5 ft (2.5-3.5 m)**

**Height: 6.5-10 ft (2-3 m)**

**Weight: 4.6 tons (4.2 t)**

**Crew: Up to three people**

**Engines: Up to 3.5 gallons (13 L) diesel, 3 gallons (11 L) gasoline**

**Top Speed: 100 mph (160 km/h)**

magnetic compass

dials and displays

steering wheel

Two huge **marine** diesel engines sit at the back of the hull.

outboard motor provides power

# Jet Ski

The Jet Ski, or PWC (personal watercraft), is a combination of a motorcycle and a boat for racing across the sea. You can do stunts like loops, surf the waves, pull waterskiers, chase big fish, or just have fun!

The Jet Ski has handlebars for steering, like a motorcycle. Acceleration in a Jet Ski is provided by a hand-powered throttle located on the side of the grip. By twisting the throttle, the driver can increase power to the motor.

## THAT'S INCREDIBLE

Jet Ski freestylers ride backwards, somersault in midair, and even go underwater and then shoot up high into the air like a leaping dolphin.

# Stats and Facts

*Freestyle jet skiers invent their own stunts!*

**Kawasaki STX-15F**

**Maker:** Kawasaki

**Length:** 10.2 ft (3.1 m)

**Width:** 3.9 ft (1.2 m)

**Height:** 3.2 ft (1 m)

**Dry Weight:** 728 lbs (330 kg)

**Crew:** Rider, two passengers

**Engine:** 1 L, 4 cylinder, gasoline

**Top Speed:** 65+ mph (105+ km/h)

Jet Ski competitions are held all around the world. Riders earn points by twisting and turning around buoys and performing stunts.

# Supercarriers

A supercarrier is a "floating city" built for war. Apart from providing a base for jet fighters and helicopters, it is also armed with its own missiles, guns, torpedoes, and other weapons. It is filled with radio antennas and radar to detect the enemy.

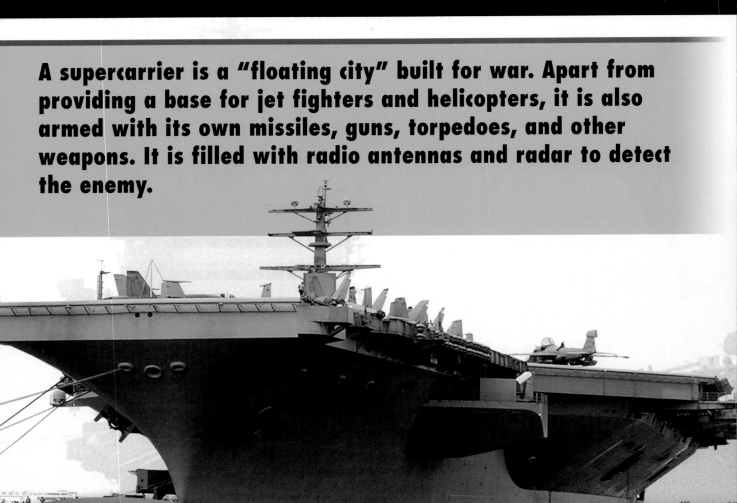

Supersized aircraft carriers are among the world's biggest ships. The deck is wide and flat, and the **bridge** (control room) tower is on one side, so planes can take off and land.

With an earsplitting roar, the plane takes off from the **deck** into the air.

# Stats and Facts

## THAT'S INCREDIBLE

You could fit four soccer fields onto the deck of a supercarrier—but you'd lose a lot of soccer balls overboard!

Patrol aircrafts on board the supercarrier

**Nimitz Class Supercarrier**

**Nation:** USA

**Length:** 1,092.5 ft (333 m)

**Width:** 249.3 ft (76 m)

**Weight:** 100,310 tons (91,000 t)

**Crew:** 3,200 on the ship itself; 2,500 tend to the aircraft

**Aircraft:** 90

**Engines:** 2 A4W nuclear reactors, 4 steam turbines

**Top Speed:** 35 mph (56 km/h)

*Radar* screens show the position of ships and aircraft in the area.

# Nuclear Attack Subs

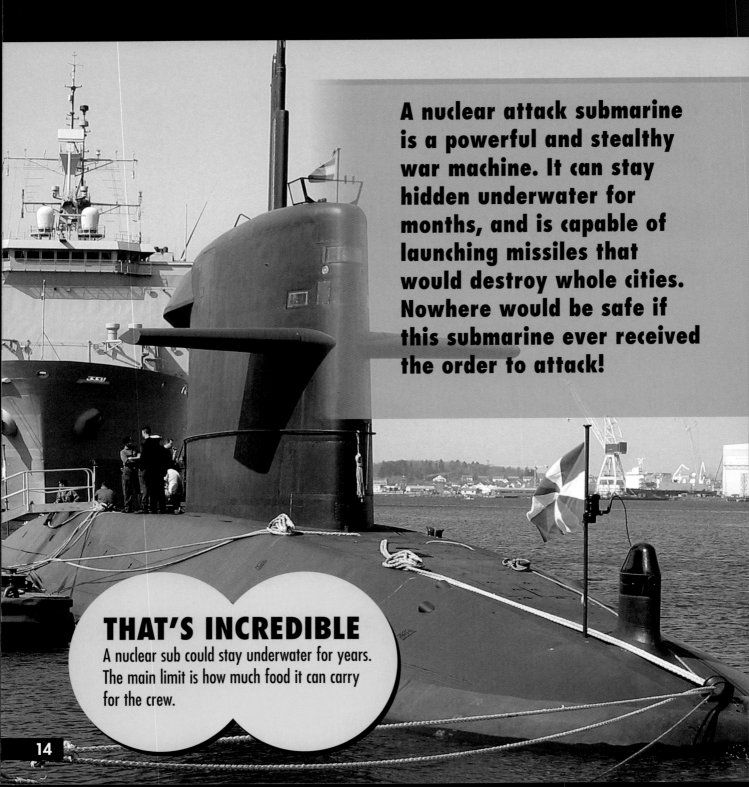

A nuclear attack submarine is a powerful and stealthy war machine. It can stay hidden underwater for months, and is capable of launching missiles that would destroy whole cities. Nowhere would be safe if this submarine ever received the order to attack!

## THAT'S INCREDIBLE

A nuclear sub could stay underwater for years. The main limit is how much food it can carry for the crew.

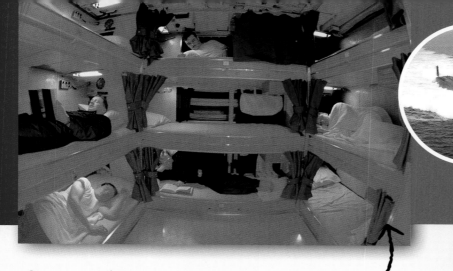

Space on board is cramped, so you have to get along with other crew members!

**Seawolf Class SSN21**

**Maker: USA**

**Length: 354.3 ft (108 m)**

**Width: 40 ft (12.2 m)**

**Weight: 10,075 tons (9,140 t)**

**Crew: 116 people**

**Engine: GE PWR S6W nuclear reactor**

**Speed: 40 mph (65 km/h)**

**Dive Depth: 2,000 ft (610 m)**

The commander and crew watch the **sonar** screen and other displays to check their position in the vast, dark ocean.

A tall telescope called a **periscope** sticks above the surface to let the crew see above the water.

# Supertankers

The biggest ships in the world are huge oil tankers. They carry crude oil (petroleum) from remote oil fields to busy ports and cities. The oil is turned into hundreds of products we use every day, from gasoline to plastics to paints.

The bridge and control equipment, and the rooms where the crew relax, eat and sleep, are all near the rear of the supertanker. They are above the main deck, allowing room for giant oil tanks below.

# Stats and Facts

If a tanker is damaged, thick black crude petroleum leaks out as an oil spill. This causes terrible damage to sea and shore life.

*Knock Nevis* (formerly known as *Seawise Giant, Jahre Viking*)

**Maker:** Sumitomo, Japan

**Length:** 1,502.6 ft (458 m)

**Width:** 226.3 ft (69 m)

**Draft:** 82.2 ft (25 m)

**Weight:** 621,704 tons (564,000 t)

**Crew:** 40 people

**Engines:** 1 steam turbine producing 50,000 HP

**Top Speed:** 14 mph (24 km/h)

## THAT'S INCREDIBLE

In 1975, the biggest ever supertanker, the *Seawise Giant,* was built. In 1999, it was relaunched as the *Jahre Viking,* and in 2004, it was refitted again and became the *Knock Nevis.*

*Cargo ships* carry goods in piles of steel containers.

# Hovercrafts

Hovercrafts float like a boat when still. However, when the large propellers in the hull called lifting fans start up, the craft rises up on an air cushion. The hovercraft is then powered along the water by propellers at the back.

back propellers

air cushion

hull

Smaller hovercrafts work as **ferries** across rivers and between islands, taking people and goods quickly across the water.

Large hovercrafts are used to carry hundreds of cars across the water.

**Solent Express**

**Maker: Hoverwork/ Hovertravel**

**Length: 95.1 ft (29 m)**

**Width: 45.9 ft (14 m)**

**Weight: 77 tons (70 t)**

**Passengers: 130**

**Engines: Diesel**

**Top speed: 60-plus mph (90-plus km/h)**

Navies use giant hovercrafts as landing bases. Hovercrafts are at home on land and sea, and can bring troops and tanks onto the beach.

## THAT'S INCREDIBLE
The biggest passenger hovercraft, the SRN4 Mk3 can carry over 400 passengers and 60 cars!

rudder

A hovercraft is steered using a flat blade called the rudder.

# Hydros and Cats

A hydrofoil is a ship. It has struts that hold it up on underwater wings called foils that make it go faster. A catamaran is like a pontoon boat; it uses two hulls to float. Some catamarans are large and look like ships, while others are small and look like sailboats.

As the hydrofoil gains speed, its **foils** make a lifting force, like aircraft wings. This pushes the main hull above the water. The foils tilt to adjust the lift force.

foils

Passengers relax as the hydrofoil skims through the waves.

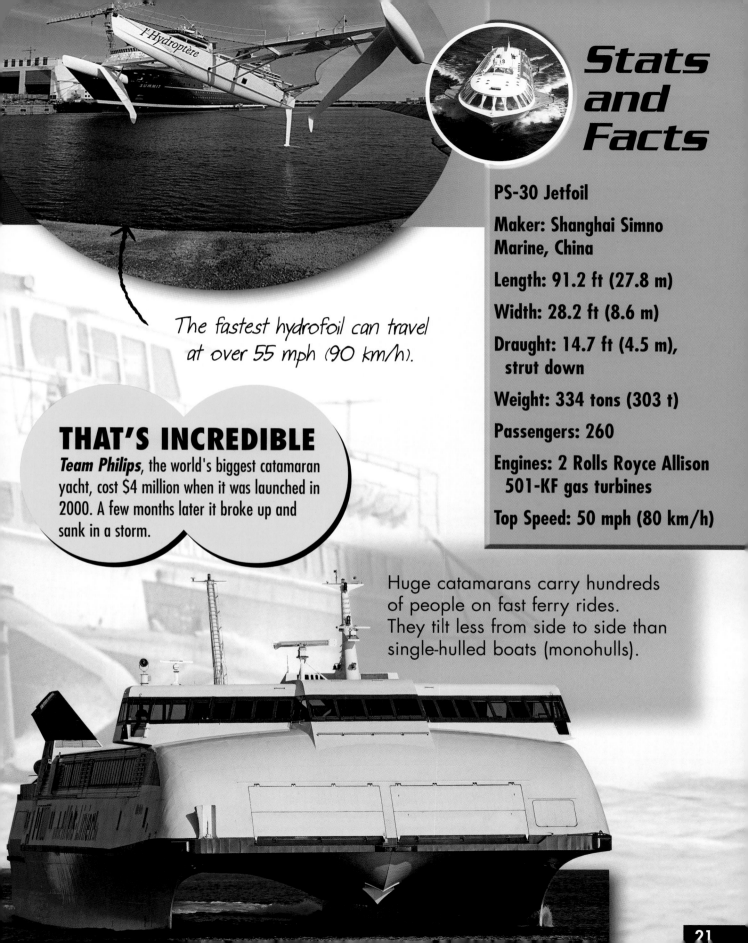

# Stats and Facts

The fastest hydrofoil can travel at over 55 mph (90 km/h).

## THAT'S INCREDIBLE

*Team Philips*, the world's biggest catamaran yacht, cost $4 million when it was launched in 2000. A few months later it broke up and sank in a storm.

**PS-30 Jetfoil**

**Maker:** Shanghai Simno Marine, China

**Length:** 91.2 ft (27.8 m)

**Width:** 28.2 ft (8.6 m)

**Draught:** 14.7 ft (4.5 m), strut down

**Weight:** 334 tons (303 t)

**Passengers:** 260

**Engines:** 2 Rolls Royce Allison 501-KF gas turbines

**Top Speed:** 50 mph (80 km/h)

Huge catamarans carry hundreds of people on fast ferry rides. They tilt less from side to side than single-hulled boats (monohulls).

# Cruise Ships

This giant hotel has cafes, restaurants, movie theaters, gyms, swimming pools, game rooms—and it floats! Luxury cruise ships are the finest way to travel and visit exotic countries around the world.

Take a dip in the floodlit pool as the fountains spray and the stars twinkle overhead.

# Stats and Facts

**Queen Mary 2**

**Operator: Cunard**

**Length: 1,131.8 ft (345 m)**

**Width: 147.6 ft (45 m)**

**Weight: 163,142 tons (148,000 t)**

**Crew: 1,200 people**

**Passengers: 2,600**

**Engines: 4 16-cylinder Wärtsilä 16V46CR marine diesels, 2 General Electric LM2500+ gas turbines**

**Top speed: 34 mph (55 km/h)**

Relax in the huge comfortable bed or sofa in one of the Queen Mary's luxury rooms. Every time you look out of the window, there's a new view.

## THAT'S INCREDIBLE

The most famous cruise ship in history was the RMS *Titanic*. She was the largest ship of her day, but sank on her maiden voyage in 1912, killing 1,500 people.

tug boat

Small, powerful boats called tug boats (far right) pull the giant ship safely into dock.

# Luxury Yachts

Picture this: cruising under a clear blue sea, past tropical islands—in your own luxury yacht. Everything you need is on board, from bathrooms and a kitchen to a widescreen TV and fishing tackle.

Bigger yachts have their own engine room with massive diesel engines.

# Stats and Facts

## THAT'S INCREDIBLE
To hire a private yacht usually costs at least $2,000 per hour. That's cheaper than buying one at around $10 million!

Some yachts can carry 20 or more guests.

**Pearl 50**

**Maker: Pearl Motor Yachts**

**Length: 49.2 ft (15 m)**

**Width: 14.4 ft (4.4 m)**

**Draft: 4.5 ft (1.4 m)**

**Sleeps: Up to six**

**Engines: 2 Volvo D9, 500HP diesels**

**Top Speed: 34 mph (55 km/h)**

**Equipment: Electric sunroof, barbecue, electric patio door, dishwasher as standard**

The main lounge has every comfort, especially for rainy, windy days when it is too cold to suntan on deck.

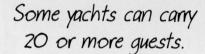

The streamlined hull is made of fiberglass.

# Sailboat Racing

If you want a month of incredibly hard work, rough conditions, seasickness, few comforts and no luxury —how about an ocean sailboat race? The crew fights winds, waves, and currents to stay on course all day and night.

## THAT'S INCREDIBLE

The Volvo Round the World Race covers more than 34,000 miles (55,000 kilometers).

At the starting line, boats crowd together to try and "steal the wind" from each other. Their balloon-like **spinnaker** sails fill, and soon they will spread out across the vast, lonely ocean.

# Stats and Facts

As the boat's sails fill with wind, it tilts over. The crew leans to the other side to keep it going straight.

dials showing wind and water speed

steering wheel operates rudder

boom

rigging

The crew climbs, clambers and scrambles among the **masts** and **booms**, and pulls on the **rigging** (ropes) to adjust the sails.

**Ericsson 70 Class Round-the-World Sailboat 2006**

**Maker: Various**

**Length: 70.5 ft (21.5 m)**

**Width: 18.7 ft (5.7 m)**

**Height: 103.2 ft (31.5 m) above water**

**Weight: 15.4 tons (14 t)**

**Main Sail Area: 1,851 ft$^2$ (172 m$^2$)**

**Spinnaker Area: 5,381 ft$^2$ (500 m$^2$)**

**Top Speed: 34+ mph (55+ km/h)**

# Glossary

**Boom**

On a yacht or sailing ship, one of the horizontal poles that holds out the sails.

**Bridge**

The main control room of a ship or boat, where the captain and crew steer the vessel and watch for problems.

**Compass**

On a ship or boat, an instrument used for finding directions. The needle always points to the magnetic North.

**Cargo ship**

A large ship that carries big metal boxes with doors, called containers, which can be lifted by cranes and loaded onto trucks or railway wagons.

**Deck**

A fairly wide, flat part of a ship, where people can move about. Some big ships have more than 10 decks.

**Dock**

A place where ships park.

**Ferry**

A ship or boat carrying people, cars, and other loads on regular trips between two or three places.

**Fiberglass**

A very light, strong material made of strands of glass-like fiber material within a plastic-type resin.

**Foils**

On a hydrofoil, the narrow strips on struts that slice through the water, making a lifting force to raise the vessel above the surface.

**Hull**

The main body of a ship or boat, with smooth streamlined sides that taper to a narrow point at the front.

**Hydrofoil**

A boat that rises above the surface on strip-like foils mounted on struts or legs.

**Marine**

To do with the sea, such as marine diesel engines, which are specially designed to power ships and boats.

**Mast**

On a ship or boat, a tall pole that holds up radio aerials and other items, and the sails on a sailing ship or yacht.

**Outboard**

Outside of the main hull, such as an outboard motor.

**Periscope**

A bent telescope that can look around corners or see above an object.

**Propeller**

Angled blades that spin around, like a windmill, to push along a water vessel or aircraft. In a boat they are also called screws.

**Rigging**

The ropes, cords and other lines that hold sails up and out, or let them be lowered and folded or furled.

**Radar**

A device that locates objects using sound.

**Rudder**

A vertical blade at the stern of a vessel that can be turned horizontally to change the vessel's direction when in motion

**Slick**

When fluid such as engine oil, crude oil (petroleum) or a chemical leaks out of a vessel and causes damage.

**Sonar**

Sending out sound waves to bounce off objects, then detecting the returning echoes to find the direction, distance, and size of the object. Sonar stands for Sound Navigation And Ranging.

**Spinnaker**

A large sail that balloons out to catch air on a sailboat.

**Tug Boat**

A small, very powerful boat that pulls or pushes much bigger boats into and out of harbors and other tight places.

## Web Sites

http://inventors.about.com/library/inventors/bl_build_a_submarine.htm

Instructions with pictures on how to build your own submarine at home, using common household items.

http://www.boat2fish.net/boats.html
Simple web site about boats and how they are built and sailed, especially fishing boats.

http://www.powerboatp1.com/
Home web site of the World P1 Powerboat Racing Championships.

http://www.explainthatstuff.com/hovercrafthydrofoils.html
All about hovercrafts and hydrofoils, including how they work, their history, and uses.

http://library.thinkquest.org/04oct/00450/ridingwaves.htm
Water transport with ships, boats and sails, and links to many other pages about different kinds of vessels.

## Further Reading

*Crossing and Cruising the Seven Seas* (Ocean Liners) by Karl Zimmermann, Boyds Mills Press 2008

*Ships* (Mighty Machines) by Ian Graham, Black Rabbit Books 2007

*Ships* (UP CLOSE) by Andra Serlin Abramson, Sterling 2008

*Warships* (War Machines) by Simon Adams, Black Rabbit Books 2009

## Note to Parents and Teachers:

Every effort has been made by the publishers to ensure that the web sites in this book are suitable for children, that they are of the highest educational value, and that they contain no inappropriate or offensive material. However, because of the nature of the Internet, it is impossible to guarantee that the contents of these sites will not be altered. We strongly advise that Internet access is supervised by a responsible adult.

# Index